These poems, varied in form and content, beautifully capture the global experience of this pandemic as well as the individual emotions and struggles that are, at the same time, unique and universal: fear, defiance, longing, grief, anger, loneliness, gratitude for time and respite, hope—and often, joy in life's small, continuing gifts. Editor Elayne Clift has gathered a community of poets whose words are haunting, moving, charming, surprising and, finally, comforting. Reading this anthology, you might find yourself saying, Yes, yes, I understand— I've felt that way too. I'm not alone.

                                       Cortney Davis, Nurse Practitioner;
author of *I Hear Their Voices Singing: Poems New & Selected*

The Covid-19 pandemic will be dissected by epidemiologists, sociologists, politicians, and historians. Now it's time for the poets. The pandemic struck every sliver of society, so it's only fitting that Elayne Clift has gathered poems from all walks of life. These writings will make you stop and think, which is perhaps the very prescription we need to help move us forward.

                   Danielle Ofri, MD, PhD, Clinical Professor of Medicine,
editor of Bellevue Literary Review, and
author of *When We Do Harm: A Doctor Confronts Medical Error*

Poetry has the power to lift us out of our current states, expand our consciousness, and remind us that we are not alone in our feelings. Elayne Clift has compiled a delicious anthology of poetry in her latest book, *A 21st Century Plague: Poetry from a Pandemic*, which accomplishes this uplifting. These poems make us smile, laugh, cry, and feel by revealing the heartaches and the unexpected boons of living in a time of plague. The poems raise our awareness, help us feel more deeply, and remind us that we are in this shared experience together. This anthology illuminates the power of mind over body and our innate power to heal. I am grateful for that.

                Michael Gigante, PhD, Psychoneuroimmunology Institute,
Brattleboro, VT

A 21st Century Plague: Poetry from a Pandemic

Edited by
Elayne Clift

Colorado Springs, CO
www.universityprofessorspress.com

Book Copyright © 2021
The authors of the poems retain the copyright for all poems in this book.

A 21st Century Plague: Poetry from a Pandemic
Edited by Elayne Clift

All rights reserved. No portion of this book may be reproduced by any process or technique without the express written consent of the publisher.

First published in 2021. University Professors Press. United States.

ISBN (print): 978-1-939686-76-3
ISBN (ebook): 978-1-939686-77-0

    University Professors Press
    Colorado Springs, CO
    www.universityprofessorspress.com

Front Cover Image by Nisha Gupta
Cover Design by Laura Ross

Reprint permissions listed after the poems

Dedication

For the health professionals, the essential workers, the bereaved families and friends, the recovered victims and all who tirelessly support them

Poetry, Healing, and Growth Series

Stay Awhile: Poetic Narratives on Multiculturalism and Diversity
Louis Hoffman & Nathaniel Granger, Jr. (Eds.)

Capturing Shadows: Poetic Encounters Along the Path of Grief and Loss
Louis Hoffman & Michael Moats (Eds.)

Journey of the Wounded Soul: Poetic Companions for Spiritual Struggles
Louis Hoffman & Steve Fehl (Eds.)

Our Last Walk: Using Poetry for Grieving and Remembering Our Pets
Louis Hoffman, Michael Moats, and Tom Greening (Eds.)

Poems For and About Elders (Revised & Expanded Edition)
Tom Greening

Connoisseurs of Suffering: Poetry for the Journey to Meaning
Jason Dias & Louis Hoffman (Eds.)

Silent Screams: Poetic Journeys Through Addiction & Recovery
Nathaniel Granger, Jr. & Louis Hoffman

Waterfalls of Therapy
Michael Elliott

A Walk with Nature: Poetic Encounters that Nourish the Soul
Michael Moats, Derrick Sebree, Jr., Gina Subia Belton, & Louis Hoffman

Into the Void: An Existential Psychologist Faces Death Through Poetry
Tom Greening

Lullabies & Confessions: Poetic Explorations of Parenting Across the Lifespan
Louis Hoffman & Lisa Xochitl Vallejos

Poetry, Healing, and Growth Series

The ancient healing art of poetry has been used across cultures for thousands of years. In the Poetry, Healing, and Growth book series, the healing and growth-facilitating nature of poetry is explored in depth through books of poetry and scholarship, as well as through practical guides on how to use poetry in the service of healing and growth. Poetry written with an intention to transform suffering into an artistic encounter is often different in process and style from poetry written for art's sake. This series offers engagement with the poetic greats and literary approaches to poetry while also embracing the beauty of fresh, poetic starts and encouraging readers to embark upon their own journey with poetry. Whether you are an advanced poet, avid consumer, or novice to poetry, we are confident you will find something to inspire your thinking on your personal path toward healing and growth.

Series Editors,

Carol Barrett, PhD; Steve Fehl, PsyD; Nathaniel Granger, Jr., PsyD; Tom Greening, PhD; and Louis Hoffman, PhD

Table of Contents

Foreword *by Glenna C. Burton MD, PhD*	i
Introduction	iii
Poems	1
Plagues *by Rai d'Honore*	3
Daily News *by Barbara Crooker*	4
November 18, 2019 *by Barbara Crooker*	5
Anger in the Time of Covid *by Thomas R. Smith*	6
The Long Summer *by Thomas R. Smith*	7
Early Days *by Irene Sherlock*	8
Lockdown Days, Early Spring 2020 *by Miriam Weinstein*	9
Making a Garden While the World Falls Apart *by Anna Citrino*	10
The End of Summer 2020 *by Judith Adams*	11
Covid-19 *by Gloria Murray*	12
Summer of 2020 *by Gloria Murray*	13
Pandemic Trilogy *by Elayne Clift*	14
Pandemic Pleasures	14
Pandemic Liberation	15
Pandemic Pain	16
Hands *by Miriam Aroner*	17
Deer Mouse *by Carol Barrett*	19
Morning Assault *by Norm Baxter*	21
Tiny Terror *by Norm Baxter*	22
Nearness *by Michael Bosworth*	23
Plague Litany *by John Bradley*	24
Remote Spring *by Sue Crouse*	25
Villanelle 2020 *by Gabriela Brand*	26
The Invisible Enemy *by D. C. Buschmann*	27
What We All Want *by D. C. Buschmann*	28
Covid Diary *by Richard Hague*	29
Jogging the Loop, Unmasked *by Charles Butterfield*	30
Things I Do More of These Days *by Marion Cohen*	31
Her Eyes *by Ginny Lowe Connors*	32
Love in the Time of Plague *by Brian Daldorph*	33
Social Distancing *by Brian Daldorph*	34
After the Pandemic *by Brian Daldorph*	35
Baking Cookies During the Pandemic *by Julie Danho*	36

After Months Missing the Crowded Subway *by Charlotte Friedman*	37
Oh, Covid-19 *by Joan Gerstein*	38
Fewer Cars, More Birdsong *by Melanie Green*	39
Metamorphosis in the Unseasonable Season of Dis-ease *by Jo Hausam*	40
Lockdown *by Brother Richard Hendrick*	42
Okay Right Now *by Roxy Hornbeck*	44
Riddle *by Paul Hostovsky*	45
Face Mask *by Paul Hostovsky*	46
Tomorrow was Yesterday *by J. Kates*	47
This Moment *by John Krumberger*	49
Space *by Sandra Larson*	50
Driving to the Lek in the Pandemic *by Joel Long*	51
Virus *by Joel Long*	52
That's What Happens *by Lynn Martin*	53
The Watch *by Pamela Mitchell*	54
Morning in the Time of Plague *by Michael Moos*	55
A Magnolia Bedsit *by David Olsen*	56
Are You Lonely or Bored Tonight? *by Marge Piercy*	57
Suffocating in Routine *by Marge Piercy*	58
You're Exhausted Because of *by Burt Rashbaum*	60
The 11th Plague *by Burt Rashbaum*	61
Quarantine *by Jennie Reichman*	62
Distance *by Kathryn Sadakierski*	63
Covid-19 *by Frank Salvidio*	64
Ode to Covid-19 *by Mary Harwell Sayler*	65
Not the Apocalypse I Was Expecting *by Karen Schubert*	66
After 'Story' by Richard Blanco *by Stephanie Shafran*	67
To Give Thanks *by Lali Sri*	69
Shut-In *by Lali Sri*	70
What If I Admitted I Like It *by Alison Stone*	71
America Hunkers Down *by Alison Stone*	72
Discarded Glove *by Vincent Tomeo*	73
Pandemic Blues *by Vincent Tomeo*	74
The New Bucolic *by Moira Trachtenberg*	75
Like No Other Suicide *by Moira Trachtenberg*	76
Covid Times in Prison *by Tony Vick*	77
Novel Virus *by Daniel Williams*	78
When This is Over *by Mary-Lane Kamberg*	79

Acknowledgments 81
Contributor Biographies 83
About the Editor 91

Foreword

The Covid-19 pandemic left no one untouched. Whether a patient, family member, friend, frontline worker, healthcare provider, or observer of the human condition, we have suffered the effects of a terrifying virus as it spread across the country and the world.

In its wake, we comforted friends, family, co-workers, and others as we struggled with isolation, anxiety and fear, financial worries, and the daily demands of our lives, all within the context of a healthcare crisis none of us could have imagined. Most of us knew, of course, of the 1918 pandemic but none of us could have realized what it was like to live through it.

Those of us in the healing professions struggled mightily to help our patients and the people close to them as we fought off our own fears and fatigue. Many of us held the hands of dying patients, wept at the end of twelve-hour days that seemed never to end, and wondered how we would all survive the tsunami that had washed over us. Somehow, we kept going.

Some of us found solace in the stories we heard or shared on our collective journey. They gave us a place of hope, sometimes wrapped in anguish but always comforting. They proved to be therapeutic in their honesty and empathy. They told us we were resilient, courageous, heartwarmingly human.

Throughout history and across all cultures, stories have helped us to cope in challenging times, and to understand the world around us. They help us recognize our universal emotions and common humanity. Stories—whether told through poetry and literature, art, music or dance—help us endure and survive.

This anthology of carefully crafted poetry is part of that tradition. It brings those of us who have lived with the Covid pandemic comfort and records for history what it was like to have experienced our century's most profoundly difficult health crisis. More important, it offers a remembrance.

I am deeply grateful to Elayne Clift for her contribution to the literature of the Covid pandemic. She has compiled a remarkably diverse set of poems that will remind us, and future generations, of a time that challenged us all.

Glenna C. Burton, MD, PhD
Recipient, American College of Psychiatrists Laughlin Fellowship for significant contribution to the field of psychiatry

Introduction

Like the Covid-19 virus, poetry related to the pandemic has flourished. This anthology adds to the literature of the pandemic in unique ways, capturing some of the best poetry on the topic in a moving, diverse, and empathetic collection that includes noted writers and award-winning poets.

Contributors are wide-ranging. From well-known writer Marge Piercy to an Irish Franciscan brother, a prison inmate, an Indian poet, a geriatric care nurse, artists and educators, the poetry speaks to challenging times in which we must find our strengths and forgive our foibles.

International in scope, this collection offers validation, comfort, and support to those who have struggled with pandemic restrictions, sometimes with humor and always with compassion. Poems address coping with mundane acts of daily life, profound emotions inherent in the challenges we have been called upon to face during a frightening time, isolation, lack of physical intimacy, and ever-present anxieties. Offering perspectives derived from personal experience, poets from various cultures and age groups contribute to the literature of healthcare crises in deeply meaningful ways.

There are 53 poets and 70 poems in this collection. Works range from the poignant to the practical. Ginny Lowe Connors, writing from the imagined perspective of an ICU nurse in "Her Eyes," sees patients, "Above the mask, behind the face shield, eyes huge, red-rimmed, gritty, glassy." Brian Daldorph considers "Love in the Time of Plague," as a couple "sit on the beach together" although "they've been told not to do it, to keep distant, to wear protective clothing." Scholar Rai d'Honoré contemplates prior plagues, including "The Black Death ... As nasty a death as can be..." Burt Rashbaum remembers being virus exhausted: "The simplest things: do I really need celery, how much dog food is left, is that a dry cough or do I just need a glass of water."

It falls to poets and writers to capture the life, and death, experiences of a wide range of humanity, reflecting in words well chosen what others feel but cannot express. This anthology offers a sanctuary of carefully crafted language that provides comfort and solidarity with others who have carried on in virtual community, shared extraordinary circumstances and coped collectively with difficult times.

The works in this collection bear witness and give universal meaning to shared experience. They help us remember, reflect, reconcile, and rejoice in small pleasures and new insights. They are each a story in verse, carefully composed, to create word monuments that quiet and comfort. In that way, they become gracefully therapeutic and healing while recording for future generations what it was like during a 21st century pandemic.

Elayne Clift
February 2021

Poems

Plagues
Rai d'Honore

The Black Death it was called, the bubonic plague,
As nasty a death as can be,
From India, Persia, and Africa,
It sailed across the sea.
On the back of rats, so quickly passed,
By the bite of an infected flea,
The lymph nodes swelled, the pustules grew,
The disease on a rapid spree.

When the enemy came,
And flew under the doors,
People quickly shuttered their stores,
Remaining fearful within.
They shook and quaked to contemplate,
It had been caused by mortal sin,
For thirty days no ships appeared,
Forty for quarantine.

Now that a new plague has arrived,
No one can be sure of their fate.
An invisible virus spreading itself,
As it learned to quickly mutate,
Tests were few, cures obscure,
Vaccine for many too late,
We masked ourselves, stayed indoors,
Prepared for a very long wait.

Plagues, plagues,
There have always been plagues,
Not easy to combat, yet we endure,
And pray "no more,"
As so many have done before.

Daily News
Barbara Crooker

And so this day is like every other,
beginning with coffee and ending
with wine. But with nowhere
to go, and nothing to do, I'm
going to take my time, sit
in the morning sun and savor
the darkness, black and bitter.
In the larger world, terrible
things continue to happen.
Here, the only action
is the hummingbird zipping
and sipping sugar water,
jazzed on sweetness, in love
with the sun. In the herb
garden, lavender, rosemary,
sage, thyme release their scents
as the heat rises. The implacable
sky is laid down with a paint roller.
Schedules and deadlines no longer
matter. If a small chore needs
to be done, we do it; there is
no later, only now. We miss
our friends, see our neighbors
only at a distance. There isn't
any news to share. The sun
traverses the sky, the day
passes, just like the one before.
Soon, shadows will lengthen,
and the stars will print
their reports in the dark,
which echoes the consolation
of wine filling my glass. I
remember to thank the grapes,
crushed on my behalf.
Tomorrow, we'll do this
all over again.

November 18, 2019
Barbara Crooker

I didn't know it then, but this was the last good day.
I was in the glittering city, visiting an old friend.
We walked on a busy street to the 9-11 Memorial,
the gold of late November reflected in the glass
windows, the water's mirror. Ate dinner
in a crowded restaurant, so close to the next table,
we could have joined their conversation. Traded
bites of pumpkin tortellini, scallops in wine,
shared a crême brulée. Sipped a bit of wine
from each other's glass. Rode the subway.
Grabbed the last two seats for a sold-out show,
then strolled Times Square, bathed in the neon
glow. We didn't realize then that these were things
we would not do again. That life would become:
An Emergency Room, An Isolation Ward,
An Abandoned Mall, A Shuttered School.
That this was as good as it would ever get,
and that the rest was silence.

Anger in the Time of Covid
Thomas R. Smith

At the city yard waste dump, I heft
sodden leaf bags from the back of our car.
They've sat on the lawn too long, killed
square yards of grass where I piled them.
Others are driving up to unload
grass trimmings and tree branches. I'm jumpy
when someone pulls up too near, feel a twinge
of something like cold anger that takes me
aback. Is this who I want to be?
Is this who the times are making me?
A perfectly friendly man has stopped
to see what's been dragging under his car
(a slender stick). Driving home, I notice
three younger people—in their twenties
I'd guess—gathered too close around the back
of a pickup, none of them wearing masks.
A handsome young man is laughing. I feel
fear for him, and then the anger again
at this group's lack of self-protection.
But I'd be lying if I didn't also
say that I feel some envy for the easy
camaraderie of youth these blithe
ignorers are enjoying. Oh, young strangers,
be well in these times I fear are starving
our most basic human sympathies!

The Long Summer
Thomas R. Smith

Nineteenth of June. It's going to be a long
summer. All of our seasonal celebrations
cancelled or gone virtual, home-bound,
the question becomes what to do with the space
we confront when we turn away from
our devices, does our time explode
or implode? There are abysses in
the hours we take great pains to avoid,
whole emotional Mariana Trenches
of memory and apprehension that can
be worked around only by staying
insanely busy. For some this way
indeed lies madness, spreading outward
from the top like venom from a snakebite.
But others, it's likely, may look back
on this as the summer that stretched beyond
the parentheses of Memorial Day
and Labor Day to become a world
unto itself in which we rediscovered
and perhaps were able to keep for a while
the riches of expanse and dreaming
we'd so often and yearningly recalled
but failed to grasp, glimpse them as we might
in the clouded playroom mirror of childhood.

Early Days
Irene Sherlock

The first weeks we took to our homes—businesses shut, schools cancelled. I woke tired, kept distant in supermarkets, waved to others on the road. No more in-person sessions. I zoomed on laptop to meet the man with three kids who just lost his restaurant job, his digital face, freeze-framed. Also, the woman who like me, lives alone. Her mother, ninety, confused without her daughter's weekly visits. Another client, a teenager, moved her iPhone around her room, *Watch this, Doc* (even though I am not that), showed off a thousand-piece puzzle, sorted by color, pattern; the assembled border, an unknown skyline.

I slept a full night after I turned off the news and played Yo-Yo Ma, the Beatles. No eye exam or lunch date. Instead, I purged files, sorted cooking magazines, unread for years. I cooked beans in simmering ham, thyme, ate by candlelight, the table set with cloth and wine.

By day, I sought the guarantee of my yard, dragging wheelbarrows of mulch that I spread with bare hands. Delicate green shot up from the lawn and in the second week, I arranged cut branches that bloomed forsythia. I made salad of dandelion greens and after the bird bath was cleaned, watched the tit mouse bathe and drink from the ceramic bowl.

Today, I zoomed with a client sitting in her kitchen by an open door. Yesterday, her daughter's hamster died and after tears and a backyard ceremony, her child opened up Monopoly. Her grown son put down his cell. The microwave hummed and they waited for popcorn. Then her husband, who'd travelled for years, rolled dice across a colorful board. I listened as outside a wren or skylark or maybe a robin sang from beyond an open widow, its repetition clear, familiar. Was it coming from my yard or hers? I listened, hoping to learn more.

Lockdown Days, Early Spring 2020
Miriam Weinstein

Before this king of viruses came to power,
her mother reminded her daily during phone calls,
I'm 96. Now she reminds her, *the hospital won't*

treat me if I catch coronavirus. Too old. An easy
target for this novel illness. Why waste
a ventilator?

The path by the creek, more popular these days
with gyms closed. A few weak smiles greet her,
some voices mutter *hello.* Rarely do eyes meet;

most look off in the distance or down at the ground.
People move to the edge of the path or pile of leaves
beside it to pass. We mustn't get too close.

This is what she feels and fears. The distance, not
the virus itself. The stepping away. The incessant
hand washing. After each time she touches

her iPhone or a door knob? Washing packages
she purchased at the grocery store? This far
she refuses to go, but the checking of numbers

preoccupies her. Generally uninterested in daily
stats, now each morning she notes the uptick.
The confirmed cases, the sick, the dying, the dead.

Birds know spring is here though bits of snow still lie
crusted on flower beds. Time to stake out territory,
robins have returned north. Strutting down sidewalks

and on lawns, wild turkeys arrive out of nowhere,
peck at the ground. Males announce themselves;
with tightly fanned tails they circle females.

Making a Garden While the World Falls Apart
Anna Citrino

It's cloudy, gray and cold this spring—
the view outside obscured. Sunny days
disappear into dismal ones.

Across the world the virus death tolls rise,
millions of stories, and griefs
hidden behind statistics.

Doctors, nurses, singers, postal workers,
veterans, artists, grocery store clerks,
teachers and students, gentle or angry,
lonely and bright, old and young, shut-ins
and athletes, the billions on poverty's blade—
all are vulnerable.

Amidst grief we go into our gardens,
dig into old earth, replenish beds
with new compost, plant seeds.
Each day we peer into the soil hoping
new seedlings have made their way
into light. We make note of what flourishes,
who needs care, what we need to do next.

Watering, pulling weeds, coaxing growth.
So much depends on taking care of our gardens.

The End of Summer 2020
Judith Adams

The trees are unaware of our dread of winter's isolation,
As warm air behind mist sends in a chill from the sea.
With covered smiles, we have not touched each other,
For so long now, though we have greeted
The runner in front of the house, and
Nodded to the postman whose job is at stake.
If there is a Lord God, what might she say?
Go buy something for yourself, and for someone else,
A coat stuffed with goose down, hat and gloves,
Include silk underwear, for others too.
As winter approaches,
Your ally is the parks, rails to trails,
and local walks.
Set up on your balconies a small
Heat source to look at the moon's
Lack of preference. Then be businesslike.
Call for a convention of wild animals
So you can listen to their sorrow.
Ask forgiveness for history.
If you don't know what you are here for,
sleep on the edge of the sea and let it
Breath for you.
One day you will be able
To kiss again. It will be different,
Pain purifies the heart. But you will
Kiss again, without ulterior force.
The end of summer is a new election.
Let the wind enter the garden bearing a ballot,
As apples and pears drop into your hand.
Holding their ripeness, their willingness to let go.
Their desire to nourish is all the politics you need.

Covid-19
Gloria Murray

now, when the hours stretch out like desert sand
or mounds of snow across mountains of days
this is the time to tell how it came about—that year of 2020
how it shook us like a giant fist belonging to a beast
or vengeful god and how the radio, the TV, emails, spoke
of nothing else but that time, Covid-19—first in China, then globally—
slipped unseen into the cosmos, then down deep into
our lungs to steal from us the breath of life, sending our planet
spinning on its axis, taking our loved ones with a sudden sweep

now we don masks, surgical gloves, rush through super
markets, pharmacies, trembling hands sticky from sanitizers,
eyes wild with fear, minds unable to grasp the unbelievable
invasion of this mutation that found its way into our lives
when we wondered who would survive, who would succumb
if anyone would live to tell of it so I will tell it now, while there
is still time for words to say how it came to be that the world
no longer belonged to us

Summer of 2020
Gloria Murray

mask in place
I sit on my swing
as I try to enjoy this mid-August day
which, at 10 a.m., peaks at 93

the bees have a meeting
decide to make an early appearance
the mosquitoes and gnats
clap in glee

after fifteen minutes I give up
take my Trump biography
and go inside to greet the air-conditioner
always welcoming my company
I watch CNN that wins the prize for repetition
MSNBC, the runner-up

not sure if it's Monday or Tuesday
could even be Wednesday
and I think about what I can do today
I order two more masks on Amazon
a three-day delivery promised
shipping free if I join Prime

and time just keeps ticking backwards
but not far enough
to the days of pre-pandemic
when I could run through the streets, mask free
color my lips and cancel my Prime

Pandemic Trilogy
Elayne Clift

Pandemic Pleasures
(May 2020)

Abundant azaleas, pink and profuse, brush my window,
Beneath azure blue skies hosting puffy white clouds,
As they mosey on by. Trees sway, lithe and graceful,
To the rustle of a gentle breeze, patiently waiting for
Summer leaves. A wall of golden forsythia,
And early green grass, form Nature's altar,
Beyond the glass.

A red-breasted grosbeak and a yellow finch,
Feast at birdfeeders, enjoying their lunch.
Book in hand, hope still high,
That scourges end, by and by.
When this one does, as it surely will,
May our hearts lift, our spirits soar.

For like birds, blue skies,
And springtime blooms,
Our lives will once again resume,
Changed, challenged, mournful alas.
But together, having made it through,
We will live to celebrate another spring,
Strong, resilient, grateful too,

No matter what the future brings.

Pandemic Liberation
(July 2020)

No make-up, manicures, or matching clothes,
Although I do miss the occasional massage.
No big-girl shoes, or ironed shirts, or bothersome bras.
No potluck pressure, or parties for which I "have prior plans,"
No cheek-to-cheek kisses, or unwanted hugs, although
One from a loved one would be grand.

No worries about my hair, or how I look,
Or for that matter, what I cook.
No deadlines to meet, I'm happy to say,
Except for an occasional library book,
Although, I confess, some compensation
For a class or oration would certainly
Be cause for celebration.

When this nasty bug is over and gone,
It will occasion dance and song,
And I will welcome that of course.
But while enjoying its demise,
With good cheer and libations,
I have to admit, it's likely that
I will miss the liberations.

Pandemic Pain
(September 2020)

In the beginning,
While in survival mode,
We masked, distanced,
And washed our hands
Like mad Lady Macbeth,
Hoping the virus would bypass us,
Lucky ones, untouched, safe, exempt.
Then, as the weeks wore on,
We found ourselves
Frayed and frightened,
Anxious and depressed,
While the beast grew bolder.

Entering crisis mode,
Tempers flared, tears flowed,
Trips for groceries became
A call for celebration,
Haircuts a miraculous event,
Release from house arrest.
Precious family and friends,
Risked distant contact at outdoor lunch.
We Zoomed, Face Timed, Skyped,
Vowing to carry on in Covid solitude,
Awaiting the darkness of winter.

Hands
Miriam Aroner

In this time of contagion, I imagine hands.

Gloved hands wary of touching.
Hands raw from scrubbing.
Fisted hands lifted in protests.
Frail hands, afraid.

Hands burying the dead in unmarked graves.
Hands lighting memorial candles.
Pleading hands, begging for bread.

Clock hands marking time that has slowed . . . .
Today like yesterday and tomorrow and tomorrow
farther than the mind can endure . . . .

Empty hands, needing to create something
out of nothing. We wash our hands of it,
this pain we cannot bear.

Hands painting the empty landscapes of pandemic,
weaving threads into masks,
writing the poetry of virus.
Piano hands easing our days.

Healing hands soothing the sick and dying.
Hands lifting you up and carrying you to safety.
Clapping hands saying thank you.

Hands soil-filled, turning rocks, planting seeds,
tending gardens.
Callused hands from heavy lifting.
Hands picking our fruit and vegetables,
those hands too.

In this time of contagion
I will myself to lift my hands in praise.
Instead of a handshake,
hands meeting in peace. Namaste.

Hands blessing water and wine,
breaking bread together.
Hands joined in dance.

Give me your hand; I'll give you mine.

Deer Mouse
Carol Barrett

The hantavirus claimed 637 lives, aged 6 to 83, by 2013. – CDC

Mass outbreaks are rare, confined
to environmental anomalies, periodic

bamboo flowering, increased rainfall.
The mice don't die, just those they brush

against in sleep. If you sweep out
a nest, the virus rides air-borne, seizes

your throat. In California a friend looks
out at the Inyo Mountains, gurgling

snow-melt stream. He cleans out
his cabin, sloshes buckets of bleach

on table and chairs, contaminated
floors and cupboards. Already dust

from Owens Lake, toxic enough.
Alkaline salts sting his face in wind.

Near every bedstead he sets traps,
window, crack in floor, wonders

how he'll do five weeks hence, onset
resembling flu. And now another

pretender hijacks the news. Coronavirus
plays hide-and-seek, no mouse to blame,

no spring to set. A simple sneeze
can do you in, a laugh, a shout, a grunt.

Before, we treated aching limbs
with mid-day rest, cooled fever down

with blue raspberry ice from Dairy Queen,
now closed. We sleep tossing coins,

tell friends how far we've fallen
through psyche's trap door, how dry

the masked desert, somber dance
ahead, leave cabins to mice, not men.

Morning Assault
Norm Baxter

Well before dawn has cracked,
brigades of aging commandos
form up in darkness, masked
raiders set on conquest.
Silent in the moonlight, they
shift from foot to foot
awaiting the signal to begin
their foray, to bag their prey.
Their skirmish line irregular,
clutching meager equipment,
unfit for a siege, ready for a
quick raid when the Field Marshall
calls for their assault, and
scampering into the light
they charge into the aisles, the
mobile infantry of shopping carts
snatching the prize, a single
twelve pack of toilet paper, a
conquest undreamed of by Caesar,
who settled for a sponge on a stick,
and was glad of it!

Tiny Terror
Norm Baxter

A tiny terror sprung loose
changed the rhythm of life
in a rush to snare its host.
Engines of prosperity, frauds
assembled on the crushed dreams of the
poor, the sick, the damaged, the old,
anyone not white and assured,
stalled by a speck of life,
infinitesimal sand in the gears.
The blood race halted,
The loops of life's course
became lazy oxbows,
where life meandered,
stopped for a long talk,
found time in an eddy.
In that arrested moment, a holy
pause as Gaia drew breath, and just as
humanity knew the lull for what it was,
exhaled a remembrance of our mortality.

Nearness
Michael Bosworth

In doorway what to do
Having crossed state line.
Nervous time or two
Emotions now incline.

Though furtively displayed
It does not matter how,
Before the feelings fade
We cross the here and now.

Nearness within reach
A heart-felt tug or two.
This time distance breached
Long lost hug of you.

Plague Litany
John Bradley

How many mouths have you, plague? In what tongues do you speak?
Should I kneel before you? Bow? Face my unfaithful face?
Were you born in the breath of a bird, the dung of a bird-eater?
Are you lacerated by lamentation, or does this bring you pleasure?
Must I wash my mouth, eyes, feet? Chambers of the heart?
Will rubbing the blood of a boar on my legs protect me?
Do you prefer we curse you, or speak to you tenderly with lies?
Will unleavened song drive you farther from, or closer to us?

Tell me, plague, do I move you to visit my neighbor's abode?
Will wrapping myself in pig intestines drive you away?
Will a necklace of iron nails protect me? For how long?
Should I take shelter below the earth? Behind each burrowed breath?
Will rubbing the scent of a skunk on my ribs protect me?
In what container, glass or lead or wood, should I store my fear?
Will small bells and rattles bewilder or entice you?
If I boil a crow and eat of it, will it make me immune? Or crave you?
Will you bind me to my bed if I take shelter there?

How might I charm you? Sicken you? Defang you?
Must I wash again my mouth, eyes, feet, chambers of the heart?
Will a necklace of iron teeth protect me? Would you tell me if it can?
Can you hear us panting? Our bowels, blood, lapse?
Where and when shall you perish?
Can we all gather to watch you wither and die?

Remote Spring
Sue Crouse

My doctor's hair is unbrushed.
We all hear the Supreme Court flush
and my therapist's spare bedroom
has one plum-colored wall.

From miles away,
your dog barks,
and mine runs to the door, glances
at the tv which sometimes
hides a dog inside.

Since we're fated for fever—
Covid, cabin or spring—
and we're alone
with our homes, returning birds,
and Zoom gallery views,

we can explore our seclusion
and even love
how it forges this swarm
of new and minute intimacies.

Villanelle 2020
Gabriela Brand

Each day, these days, I make the time for grief
It's not just sadness, but a form of prayer
I watch the world unfolding, turn its leaf

A plague marauding, silent like a thief
The cities stilled, a waiting in the air
Each day, these days, I make the time for grief

Autumn comes, the grain encased in sheaf
I don't remember harvest quite so rare
I watch the world unfolding, turn its leaf

Things fall apart, renew, and test belief
I search for hope, and dance against despair
Each day, these days, I make the time for grief

Because I know that permanence is brief
And filaments are fragile, prone to wear
I watch the world unfolding, turn its leaf

I ride the breeze, the stars, to find relief
Acknowledge kindness when I see it there
Each day, these days, I make the time for grief
I watch the world unfolding, turn its leaf

The Invisible Enemy
D. C. Buschmann

My fear will not
let me go outside
except to walk the dogs,
brave the grocery
and, eventually, CVS.

Because the slithering
python stalks us all
in unexpected places,
this rebel

obeys the rules

this time.

I want
to live.

What We All Want
D. C. Buschmann

The meditation teacher asked
my group on Zoom,
"What are three ways you want

the world to be different after
Covid-19 is over?"
I wrote:

>   More love
>   More acceptance
>   Safer connections

After the meeting, I let
my mini schnauzer outside
and fixed lunch.

Before sitting down,
I noticed her barking
to be let in, when

it occurred to me:
Isn't that what we all want
from each other—

to be let in?

Covid Diary
Richard Hague

The day of the long rain.
The day of not enough to read.
The day of eating six times.
The day of prostration on the day bed.
The day-doses of medicine.
The day of day-old leftovers.
The day of no appointments whatsoever.
The day of couched paralysis.
The day of slight recovery near cocktail time.
The day of *blahblah* cable tv.
The day of aggravating the cat on my lap.
The day of no doctor.

The day of death counts climbing.
The day of bankruptcies among the poor.
The day of bad headlines.
The day of old socks.
The day of gray light, followed by useless sunshine.
Then long rain again, then more rain.
Then another day just like that one.
And another day just like that.
Then another just like the one before.
Then another.
Another.

Jogging the Loop, Unmasked
Charles Butterfield

Jogging the gravel loop
I'm thinking of the Chengdu man
walking his masked twins
to an abandoned subway station
where the girls can run
on empty escalators and hear
an endlessly echoing
public service warning
to watch their step.
I do mine, though the loop is level
and its puddles are drying. Still
one is cautious on the turns
as elsewhere—
in corridors,
pumping gas,
at the grocery store—
I jog with others on the loop:
bird watchers, sky watchers
moving and not moving,
and with the father and sisters,
their masks under the chin at times
or below the nose
or flap-jacked off one ear,
their soft revolt against the Politburo
and its endless recorded warning.
I'd breathe easier, as I used to
if they were far off, China say,
but they are as close
as the masked amblers
I jog around aware
of my exhalations,
and I pull up my mask
trusting that we 're heading
for a safe place.

Things I Do More of These Days
Marion Cohen

Read books on bottom shelves.
Understand Sylvia Plath.
Read and write email.
Nap.
And look at the clock.

4:30 already, I remark
to Jon if he's nearby,
to myself if he isn't. I say it matter of factly
but I mean it happily.
4:30 used to be a negative thing.
Especially 4:30 PM.
My sister and I used to call that minute flabby.
Flabby meant not having accomplished anything that day.
Now the time doesn't have to be 4:30 in order to be flabby.
Now we can have accomplished a whole lot of anything and still feel
flabby.

Yes, 4:30, these days, is a positive time.
Closer to dinnertime
Closer to movie time
Closer to bedtime
Closer to when we have accomplished
whatever we will accomplish
that day.

Her Eyes
(An ICU nurse during the pandemic)
Ginny Lowe Connors

Above the mask, behind the face shield,
her eyes are huge; they're falling out of her head.
They're red-rimmed, gritty, glassy.

She yearns to close them. Open or closed,
there is so much she can't unsee.
It's required of her—to witness

this human devastation. And will anything she does
make a difference? She tightens the mask.
If she could walk near the river, gaze quietly at trees,

at sky. But the clouds she looks at, day after day,
float to the surface of films held up to a lightboard.
Lungs filled with confetti. Ground glass.

Fourteen hours at the hospital
and tomorrow promises more of the same.
So many people offer their desperation.

She sees the loneliness of their terror
and what is she to do with it?
One young man looked at her,

dressed as she had to be,
and he wheezed out, *Please,
I don't want an astronaut. I want my mother.*

Finally home, she glances in the mirror.
Her eyes are rags, barely fastened to her face.
They look like wounds, bandages unraveling.

She stands in her shower's cascade,
unable to wash away scenes she's witnessed,
fears she's felt, all the things she cannot fix.

Love in the Time of Plague
Brian Daldorph

They sit on the beach together
in swimsuits, dark glasses, sunhats.
They've been told not to do this,
to keep distance, to wear protective clothing,
but the sun's shining,
they have beer, cigarettes and music:
"The time is right for dancin' in the street..."
Martha Reeves and the Vandellas!

Dance, dance, while you still have time!
If you're sick tomorrow, if you get the fever,
if your last days are in a hospital bed,
then at least you lived, you loved,
you were alive, gloriously alive!

Social Distancing
Brian Daldorph

Outside your house
I blow kisses
whisked away by the cold wind

After the Pandemic
Brian Daldorph

we shuffle out from our dark houses,
blinking, into sunlight.

We walk to the park and sit on benches:
watch children try to remember how to play.

Baking Cookies During the Pandemic
Julie Danho

First, molasses, the sticky jar dug from the back
of the cupboard, its sweet tar pausing, then falling
on sugar. Ellie's careful not to overfill the cup
since there's no more flour at the store, and when
she drags the knife across, the extra is dust, not her
usual avalanche. She's not tall or strong enough
to thoroughly mix, so I take over spoon and spatula
until the batter looks like wet sand on the beaches
where people still gather. We roll them small
so it feels like more, and so we can freeze some
for the weeks ahead. Out of the oven, I taste
something amiss, add salt right from the shaker,
and the grains come down almost as invisibly
as what keeps us home. Today, on the radio,
the Governor said they didn't have everything
to make the tests, compared it to baking without
butter or eggs. Are we allowed to be this happy?
We eat so many our bodies are heavy to carry.

After Months Missing the Crowded Subway
Charlotte Friedman

I want to go back to the crush close push press
of unfamiliar bodies, sweat stink and soft punch
of day-old powdery perfume, scent of strawberry
shampoo from someone's still wet hair. I want
the lurch lean sharp stop, *oh sorry*, quick slide-slip
of hands making room on a metal pole for one more.
Would that I could feel a stranger's Lycra'd thigh
against me in an orange plastic seat. Oh yes, I'd praise
exploding gems on a screen, small victories
seen over a shoulder and wouldn't even flinch
from an unlikely pinch. Let my eyes
rove roam over a muscled bicep, inked blue
mute red serpent disappearing under the sleeve
of a black tee. I'd star gaze at nails bejeweled
in tropic brilliance then lose myself to the pink shell
of a girl's ear, a nape's shadowy curve. I'll bypass my stop.

Oh, Covid-19
Joan Gerstein

How considerate of you to cover
the world, allow Planet Earth to heal. Oh, lethal
bat-birthed bane, imprison us at home, until
greenhouse gas emissions go the way of the dodo.
You show us, oh powerful pathogen, how to drop
pollution levels with ease of coconuts from palms.
Oh, queen of contagion, choke poacher's breath,
keep coal in their fracked holes, shutter factories
and slaughterhouses. I bow to your potent power,
wear facemasks to lessen your infection
and gloves to keep at bay your bacillus.
You, a mighty microbe of mass murder, and yet,
oh, social spreader of sickness, you mend our planet.
We are mere mortals waiting for your pox to pass.
Oh, toxic troubadour, who has escorted dolphins
to Venice's canals, coaxed wildlife to venture out,
siphoned chemicals from the seas, before we destroy
you, I beseech you: make us mind the earth.

Fewer Cars, More Birdsong
Melanie Green

Want some cans for recycling?
I yell from my steps.
He pushes his shopping cart, plastic bags
stuffed to overflowing
down the middle of the street.
How many?
Five.
Okay.
In week two of social distancing
I have this urge
to hello
everyone.

As I bring cans toward his cart, he steps back,
a sign he knows
about the virus,
says—I'm not out to save the world.
I'm at a loss to reply,
then quip—
Well, we are the world.
He grins, his face radiant.
That's true, he says, we are!
Laughing,
we hold each other's gaze—
something like mycelium
doing its work with our deep roots
connecting us all.

Metamorphosis in this Unseasonable Season of Dis-ease
Jo Hausam

>...wood was steadfast
>Even though it was hard from loneliness. Still,
>*I will wait,* said wood, and it did.
>--Alberto Rios, *Faithful Forest*

In *this,* this unseasonable season,
blighted by borers, stricken by stress, beset by pestilence,
frass exudes from cracks,
xylem flow slows,
tattered leaves blacken.
In *this*, this gust of misery, I flex, stunned, but standing.

Rooted in one place,
insulated in bark,
implanted in the singular gravitas of here and now—rock-time—
where clocks lose mastery and stringency—
I'm becoming a tree.

Distanced from viral travel, fluorescent glares, noxious exhaust of worldly affairs,
away from the infection of the crowd,
I dwell on the essential, nestle into the elemental—a primal arboreal realm.

I breathe through stomata,
suck sustenance from compost,
laze below clouds.
I bathe in sunlight, moonlight, starlight,
gossip with breezes,
mingle with moss,
freshen in the polish of rain.
I abide in rare un-trafficked air—quiet—
broken only by the wake-up call, the above-it-all, madcap birdsong.

Embedded in the sanctuary of soil, my root tips stir, stretch, mesh into the meeting-ground, tendrils of attention tune in to the live, wild, wood-versed web.

> In t*his,* this unseasonable season,
> implausible pause,
> *this-too-shall-pass* impasse,
> I'm becoming a tree.
> I wait.

Lockdown

Brother Richard Hendrick

Yes there is fear.
Yes there is isolation.
Yes there is panic buying.
Yes there is sickness.
Yes there is even death.
But,
They say that in Wuhan after so many years of noise
You can hear the birds sing again.
They say that after just a few weeks of quiet
The sky is no longer thick with fumes
But blue and grey and clear.
They say that in the streets of Assisi
People are singing to each other
Across the empty squares,
Keeping their windows open
So that those who are alone
May hear the sounds of family around them.
They say that a hotel in the West of Ireland
Is offering free meals and delivery to the housebound.
Today a young woman I know
Is busy spreading fliers with her number
Through the neighborhood
So that the elders may have someone to call on.
Today Churches, Synagogues, Mosques and Temples
Are preparing to welcome
And shelter the homeless, the sick, the weary.
All over the world people are slowing down and reflecting
All over the world people are looking at their neighbors in a new way
All over the world people are waking up to a new reality
To how big we really are.
To how little control we really have.
To what really matters.
To Love.
So we pray and we remember that
Yes there is fear.
But there does not have to be hate.
Yes there is isolation.

But there does not have to be loneliness.
Yes there is panic buying.
But there does not have to be meanness.
Yes there is sickness.
But there does not have to be disease of the soul
Yes there is even death.
But there can always be a rebirth of love.
Wake to the choices you make as to how to live now.
Today, breathe.
Listen, behind the factory noises of your panic
The birds are singing again.
The sky is clearing.
Spring is coming.
And we are always encompassed by Love.
Open the windows of your soul
And though you may not be able
to touch across the empty square,
Sing.

Okay Right Now
Roxy Hornbeck

I squeeze myself into Time, it's tight
churning
choosing
it's familiar in a never been here sort of way
"time never stops, mom"
this is an image of what it means to be okay
it's okay
I know it is okay
because I say it is okay
okay

I wrestle myself into Hope, it's porous
languishing
labored
it's all so dry that I can't seem to escape it
long enough to let the abrasions heal
"I need a band-aid again, mom"
this is an image of what it means to cope
it's how it is
it is what it is
right

I force myself into Routine, it's soothing
processed
purposed
it's the anticipation of what is known that
gives any sort of semblance of normalcy when
this is definitely not normal
"why are you crying, mom"
this is an image of what it means to be real
to be me
to know me
now

Riddle
Paul Hostovsky

It could kill you
or it could
kiss you so glancingly
that you don't feel a thing
and you give it
to someone you love
like a kiss
of death without
knowing it.
You can't see it
but those who know
say it looks like
the pearl-and-diamond
tiaras of ancient monarchs
who commanded armies
in wars that lasted years
and killed millions.

Face Mask
Paul Hostovsky

Have you noticed
how beautiful
everyone looks

when all you can see
are their eyes?
Something about

the imagination,
how it's able to
conjure a perfectly

beautiful face
in the eyes
of the beholder

facing a pandemic
and a polity
with so many unveiled

ugly hatreds.

Tomorrow Was Yesterday
J. Kates

> Homer, *The Iliad*, Book VI: 146–9
> tr. Richard Lattimore:
>
> *As is the generation of leaves, so is that*
> *of humanity.*
> *The wind scatters the leaves on the*
> *ground, but the live timber*
> *burgeons with leaves again in the*
> *season of spring returning.*
> *So one generation of men will grow*
> *while another dies.*

Like drifted memories, dead leaves
I thought I'd raked away last fall
have come back and, risen by the wind
after the springtime thaw, are all
over the yard. I will rake again,
finite, recurring work to keep me sane.

Like dead leaves gathered in the lee
of rock and rhododendron, photos
accumulate in the dining room, where I try
sorting and dating them in the weird hiatus
that marks time. Clocks have stopped,
duties in abeyance, tenses dropped.

Things will never be the same. Things are the same as always.
That movie,
you saw it too, how we must rehearse
and rehearse every act with love
until we break the spell. It will not happen
today. It happened yesterday. Hoping

it will happen tomorrow, happen
again the day after tomorrow. April,
March, then May. Each photograph
I scan and put away in a labeled file

is different. Every leaf the wind has blown
writes the same obituary of its own.

This Moment
John Krumberger

Great stretches of time, with our routines
ripped away from us.
And how I miss the movie theatre popcorn
though we're living in a moment
that resembles a horror movie
no one knows the outcome of.

Yesterday, afraid, I walked in the woods.
where a deer gazed for a full minute
as if she knew me. I wish I hadn't
reached for my camera but
I thought it was you coming back to me.

I cried on the way home thinking of my losses
and losses to come. Then a car blazed
at the edge of the freeway, no one in the car,
no one stopping, all of us remembering
to keep our distance.

Space
Sandra Larson

During this lockdown I walk from room to room
in my condo, worried about whether I have
enough room. All this space now encompasses
seven continents. Along with Italy
and maybe Spain, the United States takes every inch of
my living and dining room. Canada must be on the porch.
England is surely in my bedroom and Boris Johnson,
recovering from the Coronavirus, in the guest room.

I don't know where I'm going to put the 30,000-plus dead,
as my closets are filled with coats to stave off the winter chill.
And now there are more than half a million who
have been touched by this deadly virus, its little prickly
flower hovering right outside my condo unit door.
My anxiety rises as more people are getting
sick and dying, and now so many are losing their jobs.
My kitchen being of modest size, I certainly won't have enough
to feed them. I'm not even going to think about my bedrooms,
how many other desperate people could rest their heads here.

My car sits idle in my underground garage, I don't go out
for groceries, thanks to a son who delivers. But worst of all,
like some magnetic force, I'm drawn to turn on the TV,
only to see and hear from a man who should have been
quarantined from any form of public office.
I haven't had wine or dined with family or friends,
seen a movie or laughed thinking my world is still fine.
Maybe I can clear all this up if I just turn off the TV.
Ah, now then, where is reality?

Driving to the Lek in the Pandemic
Joel Long

Ten cars pulled up to the Lek outside Henefer, [1]
and all of the people stayed inside. It is not safe
to congregate, so families and lovers open windows,
drink coffee, stay with the ones they've stayed with
three weeks now, their hands cleaner than ever.
We've all come to see the sage grouse do what they do
at dawn, the sun finally slipping over the ridge, lighting
the cliff above the lek and soon, the lek itself, and we,
who have been alone, we who have been alone together,
afraid of disease and the body count and body bags,
woke early to see this, male birds juggling peeled avocados
in their chests, revealing them from their ermine stole.
We have come to see them fan the spikes of their tails,
each mottled, glazed in grays and blacks and whites.
The hens, plain beauties all, gray as a wasp nest, observe
bravado, sneak around grasses while all this inflating
goes on, this *come hither* that allows the birds to stay hither,
to come to this lek a century at a time and dance, seen, unseen,
but when we see it, we return to the thrill of the world,
keep the car doors shut so we can stay in it for now.

---

[1] Lek – where sage grouse dance; Henefer – town near the Lek

Virus
Joel Long

How you brought everyone inside.
How you made the body the body vulnerable,
the body defensible, the body with its signs
and inadequacies. How you gave more space
to the birds, made the skies clear, let weather
be weather however we interpret the storms.
How spring just keeps coming, hyacinths, tulips,
magnolias on one side of the street, forsythia
on the other. How the television is full of bodies,
the masks, the bags, the weeping anchors, the stories
that make the anchors weep while the numbers
like a bull market tick up on the side. How a sneeze
makes me think I am next. How I just want to drink
because who the hell cares. How I just want something
sweet, something pleasing to distract me from my body
where the story might continue, a number, a flash
on the screen beside the expert who predicts
if we stay away, if we stay inside like you told us,
you will go away for a time, and some of us, some
of us will be here, maybe touch some of us again,
put our voice next the ear, the breath near the breath.

That's What Happens
Lynn Martin

  when you are home
  alone   alone
  you start to talk
  to Grace Paley
  one minute rapt
  in her words
  the next lost
  in memory
  both of us in line
  to hear Gloria Steinem
  I recognize you
  by your high-top tennis shoes
  and words that fly
  around your head
  like glittering bumblebees
  that Brooklynese
  buzzing a Burlington street

"we have one another   now and then"

Is that true Grace
are you listening?

The Watch
Pamela Mitchell

She was a child in the Oregon Outback. Came home
from school. Her house in flames. Burned to the
ground. Angry ranchers opposed to homesteaders.

She sits now in nursing home. 95 years old. Stroke
survivor. Alone. Watching. Locked in. Pandemic
precautions. *We cannot even eat together!* she tells me.

She waves to her grandchildren who come to her window.
Mouthing words. *I love you Grandma!* Grandson presses
his face to the glass. She blows sweet kisses. Watching.

She sews beautiful quilts. Small wall hangings of landscapes.
This is my favorite, she tells me. Cerulean sky. Snow-capped
mountains. Golden leafed aspens shivering in the wind.

She strokes the cloth. Fingers gnarled with age. *Look closely,*
she says. *See those eyes in their trunks?* She shakes her finger
at me. *Watching. These trees are always watching...*

Morning in the Time of Plague
Michael Moos

You're awake early, listening to the sound of crickets
dissolving in September's grass still damp after last night's rain.
There's the ritual of lighting the stove, waiting for the water
in your old copper teakettle, its steam like a rising spirit.
A Bach concerto on the radio fills the rooms of our old house.
You step out on the front porch with a white teacup,
to feel the breeze coming through the time-darkened screens.
With your open notebook, you trust words to lead you,
no matter how great the fears, how deep the darkness
bringing us all together.

A dog is barking. At another dog down the empty street,
or at his own voice echoing from the distance.
The same distance between us, now walking around each other
in empty streets, walking toward a day we cannot see from here.
A day that will find us holding each other again.
With our humbled arms wrapped tight around each other.
Because we can. We can close that distance, again.
Not separate, or separated. Brought together once more.
Through the deeps of this darkness,
now on the other side, brought together again.
After the plague.

A Magnolia Bedsit
David Olsen

of static familiars:
December memories
frozen on the dresser,
guitar with slack strings,
incomplete crosswords,
remaindered paperbacks
glowering in silent reproach,
a clock's numerals glowing red.

Outside the window, a stylus
engraves the sky's ennui:
a few people going somewhere.
Entropy of dispersing contrails
reveals a tiring universe
winding down to stillness.

Another day in limbo.
Another lonely night
of indeterminate length.

Are You Lonely or Bored Tonight?
Marge Piercy

We balance desire and risk daily
during this plague year. Which
friends do we dare to see? Which
we can't see at all – they live elsewhere

and traveling is dangerous. They
are in essential jobs so their
health has to come secondary.
They take chances we won't.

What's the point of a haircut?
What do we really need to buy?
Who will see me in a new dress?
Zoom only shows headshots:

we can live in pajamas all week.
Without Netflix and books bought
on line, how would I get through
the days that fade into each other?

When a friend dies, we mourn alone.
A friend marries without guests.
Dinner parties are of the past.
Our lives have emptied of others.

Suffocating in Routine
Marge Piercy

What day of the week is it?
What date of the slack month?
I have a routine. I hate it.
It's just that I twitch with boredom.

At first it was only my love
and my cats, one of whom
got sick and died suddenly
when I couldn't find a new vet

my old one having retired
just as Covid was coloring
daily maps. I miss Xena still.
Now I have a few friends

I trust inside my bubble. They
visit on the sunporch, but how
can we meet when winter makes
sitting in the wind too bitter?

I have to buy books to read.
Library off limits. Haven't
seen the dentist. Do drycleaners
still exist? Parties are for fools

and the arrogant. In my freezer,
a huge leg of lamb for company
that never comes. My year
used to be marked with bright

celebrations, birthdays, Thanks-
giving, Derby race, both solstices—
all with friends I no longer see.
Will I ever take another trip?

Once fall begins to close down
our gardens, will I get out at all?

A 21st Century Plague

Aging narrowed my life, but Covid
Is my ongoing straitjacket, prison.

You're Exhausted Because of
Burt Rashbaum

the simplest things:
do I really need celery
how much dog food is left
is that a dry cough
or do I just need a glass of water
why is this silence so loud
is this finally the 21st century
the nostalgia for a crowded room
so many conversations at once
intersecting laughter
how's it goin'
no longer the simple question
but instead
how are your people
who's on a ventilator
no more traffic jams
long lines
45-minute wait for a table
washing our hands like Lady Macbeth
no audience erupting in applause
in a full auditorium
clear skies in China
opera on balconies in Italy
mountain lions on city streets
silent factories
nitrile gloves to open mail
no grand finale shouts of bravo
standing and shouting for an encore
staring out the window at empty streets
having the nerve to flatten the curve
watching incompetence rise all the way to the top
shuttered shops not in ghost towns
but populated cities
however we return we can never go back to before
whenever we land only gravity
will not have changed

The 11th Plague
Burt Rashbaum

Should I mark
my doorposts this year
so the Dark Angel
passes over?
or will Instagram
posts do?

seders are solitary
boxes on Zoom
no one in the
same room

one new drop on the plate
as we count out the ten
plagues one new drop long past
Pharaoh's demise
brings us to our knees.
Should I join others
behind doors in fear and
ignore that Angel passing over?

are my Facebook posts shrill enough?

This isn't a seder
but a simulacrum
not enough bandwidth
with which to beat a drum

but still: all those
faces, it'll have to do,
an approximation
so vague
as we all acknowledge
the 11th plague:

Pass over us, please.

Quarantine
Jennie Reichman

This morning I am fighting through fog
despite the spring sun's pearly slant.
It will be another day of wonders
piercing the long-tolerated winter scrim:
Sunlight transmitting warmth, vegetal tang
on the wind, fecund frogs shouting
shameless desire, splintering and melting
the frozen doldrums we have
come to accept as the landscape of our days.
In the beginning there was an odd luxury
to the silent house, the injunction to stay put
that obliterated the call to action.
No errand running, friend visiting, town wandering allowed,
but the exquisitely self-contained universe of home
opening like a larder of contentment.
So many years I longed for time
like an unrequited love, flawless in the imagination.
Time proffering an embarrassment of riches
like a lottery jackpot, permission to release the imprisoned self
to walk, forgiven, in the world. Time as a birthright,
time as the shoe that fits.
But now it has started to chafe, mocks me by speeding,
meandering, plays the work ethic card,
scares me with my face in the mirror.
"What will you do," it asks, "now that I am yours?"
Agenda-less, my mind begins to fidget,
starts picking at the loose corner of a layer of stillness,
sees behind the beauty: rot and decay, the stench of fear.
The world is as it was before,
but with assumption and immunity stripped away.
Quarantine comes from *quarantena*, Italian for
the 40 days that ships were required to anchor off the shore
of Venice during the Black Death.
After 40 days, will I even want to leave the boat?
I may not want to trade my sea legs for awkward pegs
that long for the sway and roll of the open, fathomless sea.

Distance
Kathryn Sadakierski

there is so much beauty
in just one glimmering strand of hope,
a reflection of an inner dream that makes her feel less alone.
sunlight on a mote of dust, a curl of satin fabric,
airy as the beaded trinkets,
the epiphany of simple joys.
life is fragile,
hanging in the balance.
like one of the Fates,
she holds the threads in her hands,
gold silk kneaded through her fingers
like impossibly thin braids of bread dough,
the most delicate weight,
the scales equal,
for the most part, so it seems.
every option is weighed
for a woman confined;
the risk of freedom, or the safety of the same,
carefully measured days, the room in which she remains,
to roam the untamed world
or to isolate,
holding onto the table,
to what is already in front of her, to what she knows.
it is like the judgment day, separating the flocks of sheep,
flowers from weeds
among us, in the underbrush,
subject to the plagues.
will she be saved?
away from our space,
at a distance from the foreground,
she waits.
there is straw to be spun to gold,
choices to be made,
stories to be told.

Covid-19
Frank Salvidio

Eighty-seven years old with heart disease,
As if created for these very times
To walk alone, to stumble, cough and sneeze;
To calculate and number out new rhymes
For just one sonnet more, and try to say
Again what has been said already, and
Yet try to say it in some other way
Than has been said in poems now at hand.
Shall I speak of her, as I have before,
Or fashion aphorisms treating love,
Or truth, time, eternity, life and death, or
This "special providence" I'm now part of?
Be brief; but still tell all there is to tell:
A minor poet died; a sparrow fell.

Ode to Covid-19
Mary Harwell Sayler

Like dust, you spread
your virus onto us,
littering lungs
and inflaming the air
with fear
as contagious—as hard
to eradicate as rumors,
as hate, as sin.
Caught
in your sandstorm,
we cover our faces
and try not to die,
but, Dear Dreaded
Corona Virus,
you get the best of us.
You remind us
to pray.

Not the Apocalypse I Was Expecting
Karen Schubert

Covid-19's a sniper. We hide
our faces, x the calendars,
talk in boxes, miss the music.
We go missing, the trustee
who said, *people like you want us
all on bicycles.* The artist
who drew her feet,
cats, eggplants, picked off
Monday. The new grandpa.
The brother lives with
braided lungs, hikes to
the kitchen, rests.
In the night Twitter tells us
the president is alive.
We spend months
in pajama pants, cancel
Halloween, eat the chocolate.
The children, the children.
We drink whiskey at home.
We vector, die without
touching or look at morning
like we've never seen it before.

After 'Story' by Richard Blanco[2]
Stephanie Shafran

> *Before you know what kindness really is*
> *you must lose things,*
> *feel the future dissolve in a moment*
> *like salt in a weakened broth.*
> *~ Naomi Shihab-Nye*

...say the sore throat nagging at you last night simply resulted from chasing your grandson around his dusty driveway for two hours yesterday morning,

...say your recently neutered taste buds just collapsed under the weight of your anxiety and Zinc-laden tongue after sucking on lozenges every two hours,

...say my vice-like headache in tandem with your departure for the clinic's testing tent was nothing more than a psychosomatic duet,

...say the stultifying air of breezes trapped behind curtains pulled tight accounted for my sweat-soaked forehead upon awakening,

...say the zigzag pattern of my symptoms meant that only the lightest of viral loads rummaged through my blood vessels before collapsing in exhaustion and defeat,

...say tomorrow morning's first sip of juice tickles your taste buds with its citrus zing,

...say by Sunday we find ourselves pedaling easily up the hill by the jetty where I learned to swim as a girl,

...say this double-crossing rehearsal in dread leaves us sighing with relief,

---

[2] "Story" by Richard Blanco inspired this poem. It was published in *The Atlantic*, June 2020.

...then what will become of your needling dread—lungs gone awry, breath a gasping prisoner to a ventilator?

...then, instead of sniping by habit first thing in the morning, will I remember to adhere to the note I've affixed on the bathroom mirror: *be nice*?

...then will the echo of that squabble I instigated stop ringing so loudly in my ears?

...then, your hand squeezing mine, might we wade step by step into the swirling waters of intimacy?

To Give Thanks
Lali Sri

I beat the drum at dusk.
Nani bangs a pot with a wooden spoon,

and an old fisherman sings from the flat tin roof
of his hut down by the water's edge,

his voice resonant with oncoming night.
We are on lockdown in an ailing village,

this world one of strange new contagion
that closes up lungs and shuts down the heart.

Our doors are latched, but at dusk we throw
open the shutters to shout our thanks

for the ones who risk their lives and care
for the ill and fallen. We have no known cure.

I beat the gourd drum stretched by a village boy,
hope his aging mother never ails.

There is no difference between us.
We will all meet death one day. When?

The bonging of a huge bronze bell rises
from the pink temple that stands empty

down the road. Why wait to know the one you love
these odd days that keep us apart from the bilva trees,

at this hour when we run short on butter and rice?
Down by the backwaters, reeds hum

and the fisherman sings. This orchestra is lucky
to breathe for one more airy blue night.

Shut-In
Lali Sri

Six months on lockdown,
I have survived
unbolting the door only
to dump the trash,
or take in a taped-up
box of vegetables, dry goods.
Gratitude to they who deliver—
the pantry stashed with grits,
long grain rice and yellow-eyed beans.
This is month six of doors closed.
A million COVID dead
around the world.
I remember an afternoon
in early May, last year.
The sun turned to gold
as we ran through tall grass,
filled a basket
full of yellow-petaled
dandelions. You and I
set the blooms to dry for tea
in the old oak cabinet
that still smells of June
lavender flower. Days later,
we tugged open the doors,
peered into the darkness
looking to sift
dry petal from stem.
Instead, we found
the feathery heads of flowers
undaunted and
ready to seed the field.

What If I Admitted I Like It
Alison Stone

Not illness and death, of course.
Not people bankrupt and starving,
not the bills I have no way to pay.
Not the crisis, but the quiet—
my dog and I alone on clean dawn streets.
My teen daughters home for every meal.
Time at night to look for patterns in the stars.
Can we keep some of this when businesses open?

or will we barrel forward, even faster than before
to make up for lost time?
Will the lions taking naps on roads
fade into myth along with neighbors
joined in song, the smog-gray sky
turned back to its true blue?

America Hunkers Down
Alison Stone

Hands scrubbed till they bleed.
School replaced with videos.
Carts crammed with toilet paper and guns.

Yearning for basketball, friends' hugs,
the gym, we grumble in the space
between denial and loss.

Italian doctors warn
that arrogance protects
as well as prayer.

Soon, the hospitals
past capacity.
The old left to die.

The smog cloud over China's
Gone, the canals of Venice
bloom with dolphins and swans.

Will we
lean from balconies
and fill the sky with song?

Discarded Glove, Memorial Day 2020
Vincent Tomeo

In a cemetery,
where dignity lies in repose,
on a grave one discarded, blue, wrinkled, rubber glove,
degraded hallowed ground. Until a bird snatched it.

Pandemic Blues
Vincent Tomeo

I do not listen to the news anymore.
Afraid to go to the dentist.
Dread going food shopping.

In isolation so long, I do not clean the house.
Who will see?
Who will care?
Who will visit?

Please do not come near me.
Excuse me, I am looking for my mask.
Excuse me for not shaving.
Excuse my tattered clothes.

Excuse me as I write a poem.

The New Bucolic
Moira Trachtenberg

A couple clad in surgical masks
Painted little boy blue set

against a grassy sheepless expanse
of dun still dreaming of green

bounded by split rails
tumbled stones, lichen-laced

and an invisible line stretched
two yards between he and she

No hands held, but a befuddled dog
trots back and forth, unpetted

The shrubs blare yellow and red alerts
The trees yet hard and bare and bleak

We watch them skirt the edges
of others' safe spaces, call the dog close

We balance between chill and warmth
Adjust layers of fleece—on, and off again

There being no zone of comfort
in this too-cool, hardscrabble spring

Like No Other Suicide
Moira Trachtenberg

I walk outside and I breathe
without a mask
I breathe deeply in
and out
while I cycle
on a too narrow path
where a hundred others have passed
and I touch
I touch every cardboard *boîte*
and every taut plastic surface
in sight
as I walk through aisles
at the grocery
carefully choosing milk
and cookies to go with
-without gloves-
and I am tempted to lick
my fingers
but not now, only later
at home
as that dipped cookie drips
white
and I kiss
I kiss you like nobody's business
(because it isn't)
even though I know you have talked
to at least one other person
today, likely not
six feet apart
and I touch your face
and you touch mine
so gently
we might not even
feel it

Covid Times in Prison
Tony Vick

My Latino friend who lives in the cell next to mine, said in his small Mexican village
the poor say when there's lightening rich people think God is taking their picture.
"Why just the rich?" I asked. "Not even God cares about the poor," he says.

For many incarcerated people it's easy to believe that God has forgotten them. One bad thing after another, death and destruction all around, no rescue or real aid close at hand. Now with COVID-19, the petri dish that is prison becomes a waiting room for illness. When will we get infected?

If God photographs poor, disenfranchised people, he is also photographing staff and guards working with masks worn around their necks. He sees temperatures checked, people lost in quarantine for weeks, losing their belongings, with no way to contact family or friends.

The prison Hunger Games is COVID-19.

God has been good to me, despite my bout with Covid. He brought people into my life when I needed them. But maybe the Mexican folktale holds some truth. God doesn't need to photograph the poor and disenfranchised. He resides in their midst, loving them, knowing that we all must be free to seek a kinder, more compassionate world.

Without that, COVID-19 will be the least of our worries.

Novel Virus
Daniel Williams

Why use a literary term to describe a virus
when the adjective *new* would do?
A novel is at least a hundred pages filled
with life and love, romance and glory.
This is just invisible rats ravaging our breath.
Instead let's call it coronavirus short story.

When This is Over
Mary-Lane Kamberg

I'll change out of pajamas
wear make-up
get a gel manicure
cut and color my hair

I'll cheer the Royals at the K
dine at Q39
on Angus Beef brisket
and cucumber salad with dill vinaigrette

I'll donate old clothes
meet Rose Marie for Cokes,
my sister for lunch
return mail-order misfits to Kohl's

I'll skip Zoom classes,
take Tai Chi at the dojo
lounge at the pool
buy new sunglasses
drive through the car wash

I'll buy just one 4-pack of toilet paper
and a dozen jumbo eggs
fix a family dinner

squeeze my grandkids till they squeal

Acknowledgments

"Daily News" and "November 18, 2019" by Barbara Crooker first appeared in *North of Oxford*, 2020

"Deer Mouse" by Carol Barrett first appeared in *Steel Magazine*, 2020.

"Plague Litany" by John Bradley first appeared online in *Dispatches from Poetry Wars*, 2020.

"Villanelle 2020" by Gabriella Brand first appeared in Grand Little Things, March 2021 (grand-little-things.com)

"Invisible Enemy" by D. C. Buschmann first appeared in *Poetry Quarterly*, Spring 2020.

"What We All Want" by D. C. Buschmann first appeared online in *Highland Park Poetry*, 2020.

"Baking Cookies During the Pandemic" by Julie Danho first appeared in *Sugar House Review*, 2020.

"Lockdown" by Brother Richard Hendricks was posted widely online and is reprinted here by permission of the author.

"Ode to Covid-19" by Mary Harwell Sayler first appeared online at *Interlitq.org* in 2020.

"What If I Admitted I like It" by Alison Stone was first published online at *firstofthemonth.org*, 2020.

"After Months Missing the Crowded Subway" by Charlotte Friedman was first published in the journal *Unearthed*, 2020.

"Lockdown Days, Early Spring 2020" by Miriam Weinstein first appeared online in *The New Verse News*, April 2020.

"Fewer Cars, More Birdsong," by Melanie Green was previously published online by *Frost Meadow Review* in 2020.

Acknowledgments

"The Long Summer" by Thomas R. Smith first appeared at the Green Island Poetry Walk, Wadena, MN, 2020 and was included in a chapbook for visitors, *Poems of Hope and Reassurance.*

"Riddle" and "Facemask" by Paul Hostovsky first appeared in *Mostly*, published by Future Cycle Press, April 2021.

"Oh Covid 19" by Joan Gerstein was first published online by the City of San Diego Commission for Arts and Culture, 2020.

"The Magnolia Bedsit" by David Olsen was published in *Nocturnes* by David Olsen (Dempsey & Windle" VOLE imprint, 2021)

"The End of Summer 2020" by Judith Adams first appeared in *A Place Inside,* Grayson Books, 2021.

"Covid-19 by Gloria Murray first appeared in *Corona: An Anthology of Poems*, published by the Walt Whitman Association in 2020.

"Tiny Terror" and Morning Assault" by Norman Baxter first appeared in *An Anthology of Pandemic Poetry* by the Oregon Poetry Association in 2020.

Contributor Bios

Judith Adams is an English-born poet. She has published four books of poetry and two children's books in the UK. She conducts poetry workshops for youth and adults and leads a Poetic Apothecary at Healing Circles in Langley, WA.

Miriam Aroner is a retired librarian and the published author of three children's books. She has published poetry online and in print. Her poetry has been published in *Boston Poetry Magazine*, *Better Than Starbuck's* and *Pudding*.

Carol Barrett coordinates the Creative Writing Certificate Program at Union Institute & University. Her books include *Calling in the Bones*, winner of the Snyder Prize from Ashland Poetry Press, and *Pansies,* a finalist for the 2020 Oregon Book Awards. A former NEA fellow in poetry, she lives in Bend, OR.

Norm Baxter is a retired educator and poet. His work appeared in *The Avocet, The American Dissident*, and the *Journal of Undiscovered Poets*, and received honorable mention by the Oregon Poetry Association.

Michael Bosworth is retired and recently returned to writing poetry and creative nonfiction after a 45-year hiatus. He serves on the board of the *Brattleboro Commons* newspaper and belongs to the writer's group, Write Action, both in Brattleboro, VT.

Gabriella Brand's stories, poetry and essays have appeared in over 50 literary magazines. Her latest work appears in *New Salon Lit, Aji,* and *The Globe and Mail*. She is a Pushcart Prize nominee and an Osher Lifelong Learning instructor at the University of Connecticut.

John Bradley is the recipient of two NEA Fellowships and a Pushcart Prize. His poetry has appeared in a number of journals including *Caliban, Diagram, Hotel Amerika,* and *Pedestal*. His most recent book is *Everything in Motion, Everything at Rest* (Dos Madres Press).

D.C. Buschmann is a retired editor and reading specialist. Her poem, "Death Comes for a Friend," was the Editor's Choice in *Poetry Quarterly*, Winter 2018. She has been published in the US, the UK, Australia, Iraq, and India. Her work has appeared in the Kurt Vonnegut Museum and Library's *So it Goes Literary Journal, The Adirondack Review, San Pedro River Review, Tipton Poetry Journal*, and elsewhere.

Charles Butterfield has published three poetry collections, a biography and a memoir. A retired teacher he holds an M.A. from Middlebury College Bread Loaf School of English.

Anna Citrino has taught in several countries, including Kuwait, India, and Saudi Arabia. Her work has appeared in various literary journals including *Canary, Evening Street Review, Paterson Literary Review*, and *Porter Gulch Review*. Nominated for a Pushcart Prize in 2019, she is the author of *A Space Between*, and two chapbooks.

Elayne Clift, a Vermont Humanities Council Scholar, is an award-winning writer and journalist whose work appears in numerous publications internationally. She has published two poetry collections, two memoirs, and three short story collections, the third of which, *Children of the Chalet*, won First Prize/Fiction, Greyden Press, 2014. Her latest book is *Around the World in 50 Years: Travel Tales of a Not So Innocent Abroad* (Braughler Books). This is her fourth anthology.

Marion Deutsche Cohen is the author of 32 collections of poetry and memoir. Her prose and poetry collections include *Not Erma Bombeck: Diary of a Feminist 70s Mother, The Essence of Seventh Grade: A Kind of Autobiography,* and *The Discontinuity at the Waistline: My #MeToo Poems*. She teaches Mathematics in Literature, and Societal Issues on the College Campus at Drexel University.

Ginny Lowe Connors is an award-winning author of several poetry collections including *Toward the Hanging Tree* and *Poems of Salem Village*. Her chapbook, *Under the Porch,* won the Sunken Garden Poetry Prize and she is co-editor of *Connecticut River Review*.

Barbara Crooker is a poetry editor for *Italian-Americana*, author of twelve chapbooks and nine poetry books, including *Some Glad Morning*, published in 2019 by University of Pittsburgh Poetry Press. Her awards include the WB Yeats Society of New York Award and the Thomas Merton Poetry of the Sacred Award.

Sue Reed Crouse is a graduate of the Foreword Program, a two-year poetry apprenticeship at the Loft Literary Center in Minneapolis. Her award-winning work appears in numerous journals, and her manuscript, *One Black Shoe*, was a finalist for the Backwaters Poetry Prize.

Brian J. Daldorph teaches at the University of Kansas and Douglas County Jail. He edits *Coal City Review*. His most recent book of poetry is *Blue Notes* (Dionysia Press, 2019).

Julie Danho's first full-length collection, *Those Who Keep Arriving*, won the 2018 Gerald Cable Book Award from Silverfish Review Press. Her chapbook, *Six Portraits*, received the 2013 Slapering Hol Press Chapbook Award, and her poems have appeared in such publications as *Pleiades, Alaska Quarterly Review*, and *The Writer's Almanac*.

Rai d'Honoré holds a PhD in Modern Languages and has taught English, French, and Spanish languages, literature, film, history, and politics at universities in the US and abroad. She composes and sings troubadour-style songs and gives lectures and concerts on the culture of medieval Occitania at universities and other venues in the US and France.

Charlotte Friedman teaches Narrative Medicine at Barnard College. Her poetry has been published in *Connecticut River Review, Intima, Light*, and elsewhere. Her book *The Girl Pages* was published by Hyperion.

Joan Gerstein is a retired psychotherapist and educator who has been writing poetry since elementary school. She taught creative writing to incarcerated veterans for five years until the Corona virus forced lockdown.

Melanie Green is the author of three poetry collections*: A Long, Wide Stretch of Calm, Continuing Bridge*, and *Determining Sky*. Her poems have appeared in *The Oregonian, Amethyst Review, Windfall, Voice Catcher* and elsewhere.

Jo Hausam's poetry has appeared in various journals and other publications, including *Pentimento, Innisfree Journal*, and *Persimmon Tree*. She is the author of the chapbook *Step by Stepping Stone* (Finishing Line Press, 2014).

Richard Hague was nominated for a Pushcart Prize in both poetry and prose in 2019. Winner of the River Writing Contest in fiction sponsored by the Cincinnati literary festival "Books by The Banks" and the contest in Creative Nonfiction from Still: The Journal, he is author or editor of 20 volumes, most recently *Riparian: Poetry, Short Prose, and Photographs Inspired by the Ohio River* (Dos Madres Press, 2019) and the prose collection *Earnest Occupations: Teaching, Writing, Gardening, and Other Local Work* (Bottom Dog Press, 2018). He is Artist-in-Residence at Thomas More University in northern Kentucky.

Richard Hendrick is an Irish poet and a Capuchin Franciscan Brother. His poem "Lockdown" went viral and is included in this anthology with his permission.

Roxy Hornbeck is an artist, writer, poet, educator, and advocate. She lives in Seattle, WA.

Paul Hostovsky is the author of ten collections of poetry, including *Deaf &Blind* (Main Street Rag, 2020). His poems have won a Pushcart Prize, two Best of the Net Awards, the Future Cycle Poetry Book Prize, and have been featured in *Poetry Daily, Verse Daily*, and *The Writer's Almanac*.

Mary-Lane Kamberg is a professional writer with more than thirty nonfiction books in print. Her poetry has appeared in numerous literary journals, and her chapbook *Seed Rain* was published by Finishing Line Press in 2015. She co-leads the Kansas City Writers Group.

J. Kates is a poet and literary translator. He lives in New Hampshire.

John Krumberger has published a volume of poems, *The Language of Rain and Wind*; a chapbook, *In a Jar Somewhere*; and a poetry collection, *Because Autumn*. He is a psychologist in St. Paul. MN.

Sandra Larson has been nominated twice for a Pushcart Prize. She has published three chapbooks in addition to *Ode to Beautiful*, published in

2017, which was followed by a full-length manuscript, *This Distance in My Hands*. Her poetry has appeared in *Atlantic Review, Grey Sparrow, Earth's Daughters* and numerous anthologies.

Joel Long's book *Winged Insects* won the White Pine Press Poetry Prize, and two of his other works were published by Blaine Creek Press. He has also published two chapbooks. His work has appeared in the *Gettysburg Review, Prairie Schooner, Rhino, Bitter Oleander*, and other publications. He lives in Salt Lake City.

Lynn Martin's poetry has appeared in numerous publications including *Calliope, River City Review, South Florida Review, The Garden State, Green Mountains Review, Connecticut Review, Earth's Daughters, Sweet Annie Press, Chrysalis Reader, Passager,* and *Friends Journal*. She has four chapbooks: The latest is *Living Diversity.*

Pamela Mitchell is a nurse consultant in geriatric care in Bend, OR. Her work has been included in several anthologies including *Intensive Care: More Poetry and Prose by Nurses* and *The Healers Burden: Poetry and Prose by Health Professionals.* Her chapbook *Finding Lost Pond* was published in 2021 by Finishing Line Press.

Michael Moos has published four poetry books including *The Idea of the Garden*, winner of the Richard Snyder Poetry Prize from Ashland University Poetry Press (2018). He has received poetry awards from the National Endowment for the Arts, Minnesota State Arts Board, and the McKnight Foundation. He was poet-in-residence for the Academy of American Poets, and his work has appeared in numerous publications.

Gloria Murray has published in various literary journals, including The *Paterson Review*, for which she won an Editor's Choice Award, as well as in *Poet Lore, Oberon, the Pittsburgh Quarterly*, and others.

David Olsen won the Cinnamon Press Poetry Collection Award in 2015. His third full-length collection, *After Hopper & Lange*, was published in 2021 (Oversteps Books). A poet, playwright and fiction writer, he lives in Oxford, UK.

Marge Piercy has written 17 novels including The New York Times bestseller *Gone To Soldiers*; the national bestsellers *Braided Lives* and *The Longings of Women*; the classics *Woman on the Edge of Time* and *He,*

She and It; and *Sex Wars*. Among her 20 volumes of poetry are *The Hunger Moon: New & Selected Poems 1980–2010*, and *Made in Detroit*. She is the recipient of four honorary doctorates and is active in antiwar, feminist, and environmental causes.

Burt Rashbaum has published in literary and poetry journals, including *Contemporary Literary Horizon* in Bucharest. His latest book is *Of the Carousel* (The Poet's Press, 2019). His work has been anthologized, and his books include *A Century of Love, Becoming an American*, and *Tears for My Mother*. He thinks he had Covid-19 in spring 2020.

Jennie Reichman writes and performs songs and poems that document a life tied to the natural world and intimate human relationships. Her poetry has been published in the literary magazine *Saxifrage* and in *The Best of Write Action Tenth Anniversary Anthology*. She lives in Vermont.

Kathryn Sadakierski's writing has appeared in *Critical Read, Halfway Down the Stairs, Teachers of Vision, The Voices Project* and elsewhere. She was a graduate student when she wrote her poem for this anthology.

Frank Salvidio has published poetry in various journals and anthologies. He is the author of *Between Troy & Florence, Inventing Love: A Sonnet Sequence*, and translator of Sappho of Lesbos and Dante.

Mary Harwell Sayler's credits include over 30 books in all genres published by traditional, indie, and educational publications, one of which received the annual award for nonfiction from the American Library Association.

Karen Schubert is the author of *The Compost Reader* (Accents Publishing) and five chapbooks including *Dear Youngstown* (Night Ballet Press) and *I Left My Wings on a Chair*, winner of the Wick Poetry Center Chapbook Prize. Her poetry and creative nonfiction appear in numerous publications, and her awards include an Ohio Arts Council Individual Excellence Award. She is director of Lit Youngstown in Ohio.

Stephanie Shafran has published poetry and prose in numerous journals and anthologies. Her chapbook, *Awakening*, appeared in 2020.

Irene Sherlock is a marriage and family therapist. Her poems, essays and short stories have been published in various literary magazines, and her poetry chapbook, *Equinox*, was published by Finishing Line Press.

Thomas R. Smith teaches at the Loft Literary Center in Minneapolis. His poetry collection, *Storm Island,* appeared in 2020 (Red Dragonfly Press). He has also published a prose book, *Poetry on the Side of Nature: Writing the Nature Poem as an Act of Survival.*

Lali Sri is the author of *Atma Bodha* (O Books, 2012), a collection of Indian poetry in English translation. Her work has appeared in *Fiction International*, the *New York Quarterly, Daedalus*, and *Epiphany*, among other publications, and her poetry was anthologized in *Before the Dawn* (Rhode Scholars Press, 2019). She teaches literature and creative writing at CUNY's Borough of Manhattan Community College.

Alison Stone has published six full-length collections of poetry. *They Sing at Midnight* won the 2003 Many Mountains Moving Poetry Award. Her poems have appeared in *The Paris Review, Ploughshares, Barrow Street, Poet Lore*, and other journals and anthologies. She is a recipient of the *New York Quarterly's* Madeline Sadin Award.

Vincent Tomeo has published poetry in *The New York Times, Comstock Review, Mid-American Poetry Review*, and other publications. His book *My Cemetery Friends: A Garden of Encounters at Mount Saint Mary in Queens, New York*, was published in 2020 and received honorable mention in the Rainer Maria Rilke International Poetry Collection.

Moira Trachtenberg is a poet, fiction writer, and visual artist. Her poetry has been published in numerous journals and publications, including *Kyoto Journal, Carve*, and *Tikkun Daily*. Her work has been showcased in Writing the Walls at Hudson Valley MOCA and performed at the Emotive Fruition theater collaborative in New York City.

Tony Vick is the author of *Secrets from a Prison Cell: A Convict's Eyewitness Accounts of the Dehumanizing Drama of Life Behind Bars* (Cascade Books, 2018). His work has appeared in *Keep Watch With Me, A Daily Advent Reader for Peacemakers; Where the River Bends*; and

Turning Teaching Inside Out: A Pedagogy of Transformation for Community-Based Education. He is incarcerated in Tennessee.

Miriam Weinstein has published poetry in several anthologies including *Reflections on Home: The Heart of All That Is*; *A Little Book of Abundance*; and *Broken Atoms in Our Hands*. Her chapbook *Twenty Ways of Looking* was published in 2017 (Finishing Line Press).

About the Editor

An award-winning writer and journalist, Elayne Clift's work has appeared in *The Washington Post, The Boston Globe, The Christian Science Monitor, The Chronicle of Higher Education, Salon.com*, and numerous international magazines, periodicals, and anthologies. She is a regular columnist for three New England newspapers and a reviewer for *The New York Journal of Books*. She is the author of two memoirs, two books of poetry, three short story collections, three essay collections, a travel memoir, and the editor of three edited anthologies. Her poem "I Listen and My Heart is Breaking" was set to music and performed by the world-renowned a cappella group Sweet Honey in the Rock. She conducts writing workshops at venues ranging from conferences, local libraries, and arts programs to the noted destination spa, Rancho La Puerta in Tecate, Mexico.

For more information, please visit www.elayne-clift.com.

www.ingramcontent.com/pod-product-compliance
Lightning Source LLC
Chambersburg PA
CBHW050555160426
43199CB00015B/2665